I WISH I KNEW THIS BEFORE

LIFE'S HANDBOOK

SIMON YESURATNAM JAKKAM

Chennai • Bangalore

CLEVER FOX PUBLISHING
Chennai, India

Published by CLEVER FOX PUBLISHING 2023
Copyright © SIMON YESURATNAM JAKKAM 2023

All Rights Reserved.
ISBN: 978-93-56484-23-8

This book has been published with all reasonable efforts taken to make the material error-free after the consent of the author. No part of this book shall be used, reproduced in any manner whatsoever without written permission from the author, except in the case of brief quotations embodied in critical articles and reviews.

The Author of this book is solely responsible and liable for its content including but not limited to the views, representations, descriptions, statements, information, opinions and references ["Content"]. The Content of this book shall not constitute or be construed or deemed to reflect the opinion or expression of the Publisher or Editor. Neither the Publisher nor Editor endorse or approve the Content of this book or guarantee the reliability, accuracy or completeness of the Content published herein and do not make any representations or warranties of any kind, express or implied, including but not limited to the implied warranties of merchantability, fitness for a particular purpose. The Publisher and Editor shall not be liable whatsoever for any errors, omissions, whether such errors or omissions result from negligence, accident, or any other cause or claims for loss or damages of any kind, including without limitation, indirect or consequential loss or damage arising out of use, inability to use, or about the reliability, accuracy or sufficiency of the information contained in this book.

CONTENTS

Acknowledgement .... *iv*

1. Understanding Self 1

2. Parenting 16

3. Emotional Balance 21

4. Through My Lens 27

5. To The Reader 34

Conclusion *37*

ACKNOWLEDGEMENT

I would like to thank Krunal Shambharkar and Shoheb Kittur for having discussions with me very patiently regarding the content of my book and for sharing their experiences, which gave a path for this book from start to end. I would also like to thank my college senior Rashmi Itagi I for taking out time always and helping me with all the queries I had.

I would like to thank my family for their immense support throughout my life in a very positive way without which I would not have thought of all this.

Finally, I would like to thank all my friends who have supported me and are supporting me throughout this journey.

CHAPTER 1

UNDERSTANDING SELF

It is very important to understand about self to better understand self-behavior. To begin with, let's look at a few aspects of learning and emotions.

How often does our brain learn?

Every second our brain is learning through our experiences and through our senses.

How emotions are created?

The brain manufactures or creates emotion that is unique to a situation and is based on past experiences. This means that our behavior and emotions are conditioned or influenced by our experiences that are consumed by our senses.

We are influenced or conditioned by TV, social media, cell phones, and other people by all our senses from our surroundings.

Let's also look at some other things which are influenced by media:

We crave food while watching movies or matches like football or cricket, even when we are not hungry.

We learn various things by watching television or advertisements without realizing that our brain is learning, i.e., Vicarious learning.

Our food habits, thoughts, speech, etc. are all influenced by the media we consume.

We behave in certain ways or show particular emotions in situations as learned from the media (even when it was not needed or is exaggerated).

We get addicted to phones or certain media.

We find it very difficult to choose a path or have a mindset that is different from society.

We accept certain things as right only when it's accepted by society and we look for validation from others.

Parents mostly don't update themselves about newly available career options for their children. They rarely spend time on it individually and are mostly influenced by what they hear from surrounding people or media. They follow what they hear about what career options others have chosen or will choose.

Spending family time has become underrated. We sometimes regret not giving time to family. We only do so when it is most important as we measure our accomplishments by the money we have, places we visited, and many more things outside the home. Even society and social media help in reminding and measuring these but fails to acknowledge or count the number of hours spent with family or the number of times one has had lunch or dinner with family. When we don't remember such details, it might be because we don't address it and hence we might not appreciate it in the same way as we appreciate other accomplishments. Similarly, we think a lot of things are right just because we are convinced by society and by the media.

Now, let us look at how the media or others have the power to convince or influence us.

Generally, when someone wants to convince you, they will tell you a scenario where it will fail and will give you a solution as well so that you believe. In case, if they want you to choose a particular solution then they will tell you the same solution. That's the reason why we feel all quotes, books, and motivational talks are true even if they change their definition or modify it.

Let's understand better with an example:

We have heard the quote **Practice makes a man perfect!**

We all believe in this quote but someone can convince you saying that this quote is wrong by telling you about a failure scenario and by providing with an alternate solution. In this case, he or she might say **practice in the right direction will make you perfect** and then you will believe their approach is the right approach. This is the reason why we feel almost all the content we consume from the media is right.

Why we believe it is because it's partially right as the truth in every scenario is different and anything to happen in this world it depends on multiple factors and also the proportion of that factor.

But one important characteristic is that, if one factor is used in more proportion, then indirectly another factor will be used unknowingly. i.e., If a task requires us to work hard and if we put in more hard work then we develop concentration without explicitly thinking about using it. This makes it difficult to understand explicitly how many factors are involved in performing any task. Due to this, it's easy for anyone to pick any factor and try to convince another person. So in the above example, the direction of the practice is the factor used to convince the person.

After reading the example of concentration and hard work, many people will think that concentration is also required, and yeah, it's important but we are not sure as to how it's related to other factors. I don't intend to comment on whether it's important separately or not here because as I said earlier it depends on factors, situations, contribution/proportion of factors, an association of the factors, and their dynamism i.e., increase in one-factor proportion makes the increase in another factor proportion, which was required while performing the task. This appears to be very flexible due to which people use it to convince others to be conditioned or habituated.

Even when we know all the factors involved and their proportion used, the outcome differs in each case as this also depends on each individual. That is, when the factors interact with unique personal traits, the outcome differs.

For example, we have heard below statements from many people with regards to Reducing weight:

It all depends on physical exercise, so do exercise more and eat whatever you want.

It all depends on food intake so choose your food accordingly or eat less and do normal exercise.

It depends 80% on food and 20% on exercise. It also depends on what time we are eating and on intermittent fasting.

One meal a day must consist of all essential nutrients.

One should not skip any meal but eat less in each meal.

So what exactly should we do?

It depends on each individual. This means each individual should understand their body system and act accordingly.

Another example is, when we see YouTube videos of any motivation or strategy for excelling in any exams, we will get a lot of videos with similar topics like, **"Three ways to become successful in this exam"**, **"Patience is key"**, **"You can't clear the exam with hard work"**, **"Common sense is key to clear this exam"**, **"If you have confidence, you will clear exam",** etc. We generally believe these are due to an inferiority complex and due to other internal reasons mentioned above.

Due to this reason, many experiments in this world have been proved right saying it depends on a certain number of factors and again another theory comes up and gets approved saying it depends on another set of factors. We believe both as we don't know exactly how many factors are involved and their proportions and associations with each other.

Sometimes we watch motivational videos or interviews with successful candidates. After which, we feel motivated but sometimes seeing more positives is also disadvantageous.

Explanation with an example:

When any topper or motivational speaker or anyone who is motivating through videos or by talking about all positive while not mentioning all challenges or struggles he faced, then our brain learns all positive points about it, and when we actually execute it, obviously we face challenges and then we will feel more demotivated because our brain or mind didn't expect it. Then we feel an inferiority complex and we may not be able to perform other tasks well we might also feel less confident and may enter a negative thought loop.

However, if challenges or difficulties faced and accomplishments were told equally, then we will feel that it's common to face challenges so we might continue doing our task without many negative thoughts. This way we will develop the right attitude among others to make them ready to face challenges as well while performing any task. I also feel that we should tell as objectively as possible.

Similarly, a lot of content that we consume is unrealistic and since our brain has learned it as it receives, we feel that's the reality due to this many times we fail to realize the actual reality and this happens because it becomes difficult for our brain to accept the reality which is different from what it has learned due to conditioning or influence from surroundings and another reason is that the brain cannot differentiate between the reality and imagination. And we imagine and generate thoughts based on what we consume through our surroundings i.e., media, society, etc.

Now, let's understand with an experiment if it's really the thoughts in mind that drive us to do this in this context by thinking about our favourite delicious food.

Some like biryani or dal rice or roti sabzi or pizza or pani puri, noodles, Manchurian, etc. Now if you observe, the image of your favourite food or other food also which you read above will pop up in your mind, you might also remember a picture in which you are eating your delicious food. Images that we consumed while seeing an advertisement might also pop up.

Now you will be salivating!!!! ☺

If you think more then you will get the craving and most probably you may end up eating it for your next meal unless you have a habit to resist it or maybe you might not eat due to other constraints like it's not convenient to order or you don't have time to cook, etc. You can also resist it by thinking multiple times in a negative way that "I don't want to eat, I don't want to eat".

And yes, we are habituated based on our past experiences and yes, we can eliminate it by changing our experiences which also includes talking to ourselves i.e., brain telling positive points of leaving the habits and negative points of having the habit. Due to this conditioning, it becomes difficult to go against it and do tasks. So next time please don't regret if you are not able to do any task easily because many people think it's their fault that they are unable to do the task and they feel underconfident and go in a negative loop of thoughts. You should remember that it might take a little more time but you will eventually do it.

Many will also regret that they should have known this before, but it's very disheartening to know that even though they realize the importance of knowing this on time, they don't have time to share it with their children.

Now let us look at some scenarios to understand why many parents won't give enough time for family or parenting.

Scenario-1

They devote most of their time to achieving their goals.

They do it because we have been conditioned in such a way that everyone should have goals or purpose or aim and should work hard towards achieving them. I agree that we should have a certain goal but we shouldn't do it by sacrificing family time i.e., Ideally, we should also give time for food, exercise, and spirituality which is subjective to an individual.

Because even if we become successful by sacrificing family time, we eventually move to another new goal and the process is never-ending. And as we see in interviews with successful candidates, they usually regret not giving enough time to their families.

Why is it so that we continuously move to another goal?

Before reaching our goal, our mind is occupied with and about the goal because we are working towards it. That's why we are curious about reaching goals but once we reach, we are happy for only a limited time until we are thinking about what we have achieved. Once our mind or brain starts thinking about future goals, we start working on them and we are not in a happy state anymore unless we remember about our achievements in a positive way.

Why does our brain start thinking about the next goal?

Because we have been influenced or conditioned by our society to think about the next goal. If we don't plan for the next goal then people will ask you what your next goals are. **What's the next plan?** So, the brain learns it and we start preparing for the next goal.

So, we can say that it's all in our mind and what it contains will create your emotions.

Appreciating our accomplishments is one way to be happy!!!

We should not give all our time to our goal, instead, if we divide time by balancing family, health (and spirituality if we believe) and give our 100% in whatever we do then we can be more productive and will never regret any point of time in life. Else we will regret each time when we think about our past and analyze our life, we will think that "We couldn't give time for these and that".

If you think in terms of balancing life with family time, health, (spiritual), and goals, then you will surely find ways to balance them. If you don't think in that direction then obviously you will not find time which is the case with many people. Because many people hear from others that it is difficult to manage goals with family and health so they do not even think of balancing it.

Scenario-2

Instead of giving family time they try to invest their time in working to save more and more money for their children.

It is like, parents building a smooth path or road for their children so that they can go without any hurdles but the child goes wandering in the forest asking which path to take, and finally based on his experience with his surroundings, he chooses the path.

Money alone will not guarantee a good future for your children. Instead, parents should also spend time with their children to choose the right path. Sometimes parents tell children to do what they like but they do not realize that their children's choices are influenced by their environment. Instead, parents should influence them from childhood (maybe until a certain age to choose the right path).

So, it's very important that parents give time to children and lay the foundation or values or directions so that they can automatically choose the desired right path. If we do not influence or habituate them with the right things. When they are grown up, parents tell them to choose a path that children might not like as they are influenced by other things. Instead of being fully occupied making money for the future of our children, we should also take out time for family and should teach children to be happy even if they do not have adequate money.

Scenario-3

Lots of people do not focus much on parenting because it is not talked about more which leads them to give less time parenting as others do in society.

Until now we looked at the various experiences in which our thoughts in mind have driven us to do the tasks. Now let's get a little deeper and let me introduce one more factor which affects us i.e., **RANDOMNESS.**

Once thoughts are present in our mind, we look to do random things and that's also a reason why we don't appreciate things we have. We like randomness. I mean the reward that we get when we do things randomly because it releases **dopamine**.

Since our brain is curious, we become curious to know about a lot of additional things e.g., things that advertisers want us to think about. They also make us addicted by making us emotional and also by showing random content which makes the brain to release feel-good hormones i.e., Dopamine.

When I analyzed all the examples below, I found that it's all due to randomness:

We like cricket, football, hockey, etc. because of their random nature.

We like to talk to people who talk to us at a random time on a random day or text or reply randomly but we don't find that excitement when we talk to people who respond immediately or talk to us at a predictable time or are available for us all time. (Exceptions also exist)

Take examples of movies or serials or web series etc. We get attracted because every scene in it is random to us.

We like various dishes even though they are unhealthy because they are made up of different ingredients (which are random) which give us some different tastes.

We like playing video games because of their random nature.

People get addicted to gambling easily because its results are random.

The cashback which we receive randomly from various payment apps makes us habituated to using their apps.

We also like free things or gifts, complimentary things or discounts irrespective of their price because it is given randomly.

This is another reason we see our phones more. i.e., When we post something on social media, the company holds the likes and shares of that post and releases it randomly. Due to this, we check phones continuously to check how many likes we have got on our posts because we are not sure when our likes on our posts increase.

So, if we are not influenced, then there are not many random things in mind and we won't be diverted much.

CHAPTER 2

PARENTING

*N*ow after understanding in depth about self and why we should give time to our family from the previous chapter, now let's look at a very broad level of how we should go about parenting so that you can make your own precise level plans to execute it.

The main idea here is to eliminate the influences, but not all influences can be avoided completely so we should limit them by choosing and enabling them with those limited experiences which we think are good for them. We should also provide them with definitions for all the emotions or some stereotypical words or other words which we think will help them in a positive way.

Let's understand better with an example:

In case you want them to excel in their studies then parents should condition them accordingly. i.e., By telling them the positive points about good things like telling them like "Studying is joy", telling them "How happy it is to learn". Telling them "How fulfilled one will feel when they know or understand things after reading". Otherwise, they will listen to experience as it comes from the surroundings, which is defined as education or studying is difficult, hard, boring, it takes effort to study, etc. which makes them dislike studying and they can experience limitations. Thus, the brain also learns accordingly to the influences of the surroundings.

Let us look at a few examples who benefited from the conditioning of their parents in the right way:

The parents of Sudha Murthy i.e., R. H. Kulkarni and Vimala Kulkarni raised their children in such a way that they developed a love towards books, love towards knowledge, respected education, etc. which I got to know by seeing an interview of Sudha Murthy.

The parents of Tejaswini Manogna, have put efforts from childhood to enable her to acquire multiple skills by giving her the required exposure and supporting her accordingly.

From these examples we saw how the parents had put in efforts which made them what they are today and yes it requires good effort from parents for the initial few years but rewards will be unimaginable.

Since TV and mobile phones affect the child's behavior by influencing them and their emotions too, we should not let children consume them. It's best if avoidable influences like watching TV are not consumed at all but it is difficult for some parents as parents are habituated to media and this is also based on parent's culture, spirituality, and choices. They should at least keep children away from media consumption for at least a **minimum** number of years until they can understand what's good for them and what's not good so that children later can decide by themselves whether they want to consume it or not.

Once we have reduced the influences, now the parents should also encourage them from an early stage to read about how the mind, brain, emotions, body, etc. works so they can understand themselves better and can use that information or knowledge in performing any tasks or goal or purpose or aim.

Let's see one example of the impact of conditioning on children i.e., Regarding children's eating habits:

We usually unknowingly influence children by saying that certain dishes are good and parents make them eat more. i.e., By saying **It's good, you should eat, take more, it's delicious,** and the brain learns it accordingly.

These experiences will make them habituated to eating out of proportion and eating unhealthy too. Since health is also very important, it's needed to make them adopt the right food habits from childhood so that they are always healthy.

At certain times, we cannot stop them from consuming experiences like talking to friends or society but we can or should reduce the negativity or stereotype. One way to do this is, let's pick one general word i.e., **problem**, so since it's often used and has a negative impact, we should set our own definitions of it.

Maybe we can define it as **"A puzzle in life which we have to solve and move on."** The advantage of solving a puzzle is that since we know how to solve it, we can use these steps in solving the next puzzle. The disadvantage is that we lose time as we invest that time in solving puzzles instead of focusing that time on our actual task".

This way we should define our own statements so that even if they hear those words in society, they aren't affected as much as others.

One more important thing many parents miss or many don't stress about is making children learn to say **NO** to the unwanted experiences they get from society as it has an effect on them or when required. So, we should equally make them aware of when to use **NO.**

Unfortunately, at present society's perceptions and parent's habits are being conditioned to their children. So these are a few examples to give you an idea of how we can make a positive impact on children's life. Now after reading you can have your own customized plans for your children accordingly.

Till now we looked at scenarios to prove that influence from surroundings affects the child's behaviour so the best way to go about parenting is to limit the unwanted experiences and induce the necessary experiences from childhood when the child has not been conditioned yet.

How one should go about parenting if he or she is already conditioned by things in society?

Since the parent now knows the root cause of the problem, to achieve the desired behaviour, the parents should change the experiences of the children slowly which are influencing them in a negative way, and try to influence them which has positive impacts.

If the reader is an adult and is already influenced, then can change the experiences by talking to themself i.e., brain about what you want to do and the advantages of doing it and the disadvantages of not doing it (i.e., Positive affirmations) and reduce the surrounding influences or consumption at your own pace till it doesn't affect you anymore.

CHAPTER -3

EMOTIONAL BALANCE

*H*ere in this chapter, I want to talk about how important it is for us to be emotionally balanced or stable. Let's start by understanding the definition of it.

What is Emotional Balance?

Emotional balance is the ability to remain calm and clear-headed during stressful situations or crises i.e., None of our emotions are too high and too low when we are emotionally balanced. It is always very important to note that we should think and act only when our emotions are balanced. If they are not balanced then bring them to normal state i.e., calm or relaxed and then think and act accordingly. Even when you want to think objectively you need to be emotionally balanced.

Does emotional imbalance have any effect?

Yes, when we are not emotionally balanced then it affects or alters our perspective, views, thought processes, etc.

For example, let's remember scenarios where you had a fever. Try to remember your thoughts during fever and after the fever. There is definitely a difference in thoughts, views, etc. Or just remember a scenario where any of your emotions were high or low and think of the thoughts you had during that period. They differ significantly.

Reacting during Emotional Imbalance have any impact?

There are many scenarios where reacting to emotional imbalances could impact us, these emotional triggers can be caused by certain people as well for their benefit. I will list down some of the scenarios so that you can get an idea of where we should be careful not to react based on our thoughts as thoughts during emotional imbalance are generally not right unless we have trained ourselves for the same or we have thorough knowledge about the situation.

Scenario-1:

In this scenario, I will give examples of scams where scammers trigger emotionally to achieve their agenda.

Example-1: The scam done by scammers using a multi-level marketing strategy.

Scammers lure people by making them trigger emotionally. i.e., Because of the importance of money and the need for it makes people emotional when they hear someone guaranteeing huge profits or money easily and sometimes in a short span. Also in this digital age, it's easy to create a website and show data and convince people.

Example-2: The scam done by scammers using digital data.

In this digital age, we generally trust Google reviews but sometimes we must be careful in certain scenarios, certain places. Because when we are in need, we are in emotional so we don't see the number of reviews and we don't thoroughly check the reviews when we are in a hurry and we believe the reviews. i.e., Let's say you need a bike for rent in a city or nearby tourist place you Google it and you will check Google reviews where they mention that "bike will be delivered to your location" Then you will call and book the bike, on call they will also manipulate saying only one bike available, etc. and they will ask for online payment. Then you will pay seeing the reviews and the convenience they provide in delivering bikes to your location. If your emotions are high, you will not realize that it's a scam.

Example-3: The scam done by scammers by promising better-paying jobs.

We see a lot of online scams, a recent example is of a job where we have to like 2 or 3 YouTube videos and we get 50 rupees for each like.

Scenario-2:

In this scenario, let's look at examples where the behaviour is manipulated.

In this digital world and after the introduction of AI, through the use of user data it has become easier to manipulate the user for their profit.

Examples-1: If you are searching for any travel place to visit or if you are booking tickets to any tourist place, then you will get a lot of ads related to the same. You will get emotional when there is a huge discount available for hotel bookings. Here if you were in doubt about planning a trip, you might plan for a trip after a discount.

Example-2: This is the most important example of this chapter so I will mark it in bold. **Many people get blackmailed through online and offline modes. Let us consider a scenario of blackmailing through a phone call.** When someone threatens on a phone call then the person will get frightened and his emotions will be high and he will not be in a position to think in the right direction as the person will be highly unstable emotionally.

In this scenario of blackmail or scenarios of scam or any other scenarios applicable, the person should make his emotions stable and talk to family. If the person is really not in a position at that point of time to talk to the family, then they can reach out to friends for help finding the right approach or resolution steps i.e., Approach each one from a circle like school friends, college friends, neighbour friends, office colleagues, etc. to understand different perspectives and also to eliminate bad scenarios.

If you don't have any friends or if anyone is not helping or if any of your friends is not trusting you then you should search online or watch any videos related to that for resolution steps or way forward. **And if no one, then you can take help from the government through various helplines whose information you will get online.**

Sometimes people get threatened online from social media, here since it's online many people might have faced the same as blackmailers will target many so the person should search online for these types of scams, and mostly, they will get a lot of information about the scam online, so the person should take appropriate genuine measures and if they don't find any information online then they should follow the above resolution steps mentioned in scenario of blackmailing through phone call.

You should always remember that the mistakes you have made do not define you!!!!

After going through these scenarios, you might have got an idea about how our thoughts, views, etc. alter when we are emotionally unstable which eventually changes our behaviour. So please keep these things in mind and spread this information to whomsoever possible.

So now you have the knowledge about how one can fall into a trap when they are emotionally unstable. So please help others who are susceptible to falling into a trap or who have fallen into a trap including in any of the above scenarios.

I will end this chapter with a quote, *"Your eyes can't see, what your mind doesn't know"*

CHAPTER 4

THROUGH MY LENS

We also understand and learn various things through observation throughout our life. Here in this chapter, I want to talk about my important observations till now so that it can be useful to you.

Observation-1: Generally, parents sacrifice a lot for their children and children will sacrifice for their children and it continues on and on which I felt is not right. We do it because in society almost everyone follows the same. Ideally, parents who sacrificed a lot for their children, children should try to voluntarily fulfill their parent's needs or wishes or anything for them, equally as they do for their children.

Observation-2: I analyzed that mostly many people around us behave in a certain way as per their agenda. So, they speak and behave as per their agenda. It's good to have an agenda but it shouldn't influence or affect others in a negative way. So, as I mentioned in previous chapters that our surroundings also affect us, this is also a similar example of it, so we should make sure that their words do not alter our path. We should be cognizant of people who have an agenda and ignore their words because when people have an agenda then there are no emotions associated, which means the person who has an agenda to fulfill will not think of other's emotion.

Similarly in case, when there is an addiction then there are no emotions. This means when a person is addicted to something then he or she will do anything to complete the addicted task.

Let us understand this with an example:

A credit or debit card agent has an agenda of meeting his targets so they will give their 100% to convince another person to purchase it without understanding the other person's needs or emotions.

(Note: This is just to make the reader understand because in this example, they are just doing their job.)

Another example of our surroundings could be that some friends will call for a trip not because they want to go on a trip with you but because they can share their expenses. You can understand it because they call you randomly out of the blue sometimes and not regularly. They will convince you, maybe by telling you that, *"We should travel often because life is only once* ☺ *"* They will tell you irrespective of whether it's the right time for you to go on a trip or not. Apart from people who behave in their official capacity, if people behave abnormally nice, then we should think and behave objectively until we realize that they are genuine.

One important point to note is that there is a possibility that anyone can convince the other person based on their need or agenda but once the other person realizes sooner or later that the other person's behaviour was based on a certain agenda then the relation between them won't be the same again.

Observation-3: As I mentioned in previous chapters, if we change our thoughts, we can get away from society's stereotypes or views. I have a good personal experience of it. As some people don't want to cook because some feel it is a burden, and some feel it is hard, (not generalizing though) but when I wanted to start learning cooking, I was thinking that how magical it is to see the hard rice when we boil in water becomes soft, lots of things become soft after cooking, etc. When I had these thoughts in my mind, I was enjoying cooking. It is the same to date. I never felt burdened or hard. It also enabled me to help my mom in the kitchen whenever I go home.

Observation-4: As I observed in our society many men treat women unequally if the woman doesn't earn, as they consider money as a measuring value and also think that raising the children is easy. But as we read this book, we understand how important and how impactful it is to raise children in the right direction. So, in some cases where women are not earning, they are giving more time to their children. So, I think we should consider the invisible factors as well and I feel or know both are equal.

Observation-5: When we have multiple options, we don't think about other people's emotions and when we have a single option, that is the only time when we have an emotional connection with others.

For example, let us say you have four bikes at your home, if you want to go out then you would choose randomly anyone. So, you are not emotionally attached to the fact that "I should go with this bike" as much as you would if you had only one bike.

Let us take another relevant example:

If you have only one friend and you wanted to visit a place but he couldn't make it with you, it obviously will make you sad and also you will ask the person why he was not able to come. We connect with them emotionally. But let us say in another case if you had two friends in which you went with one friend based on your convenience on a particular day, then you usually don't think about the other person emotionally. i.e., Whether another person was interested to come or whether he will feel bad.

Why does it happen?

When we are occupied with one person, and they come regularly or are close friends, we would have thought "Why the person didn't come', etc. and our mind would have created emotions accordingly. So, when you both have a conversation regarding the any topic, it's very difficult to understand the other person when you have an option and he doesn't have any in that particular scenario. Apply in your life, you will understand it better but it will become difficult for you to be on the same page when the other person claims that he has not been invited in a scenario where you had many options.

Observation-6: I think one reason or factor we get addicted to temporary pleasures is that, if we see it, we consume or experience it. So, if we can delay the consumption or experience then we can reduce the addiction. For example, we drink cold drinks or eat junk food as soon as it's brought to the table.

Let us test this with an experiment that you can try:

If you have a habit of eating food or snacks or drinking cold drinks while watching movies, matches or any entertainment, just keep the eatables near you while watching entertainment and don't consume it. Slowly your eating habit while watching entertainment will be reduced.

Note: This may not be applicable to all temporary pleasures.

Observation-7: Representation has its own perception.

Habit: If we see someone doing something repetitively then we tell the other person that you have this habit. But we are not sure in what stage of habit he is in. But even if he is in the initial stage or if he is not actually habituated, he might feel stressed and might look for solutions to get out of the habit. These thoughts may lead to more negative thoughts. The reason for thinking this is because each representation it comes with certain perceptions i.e., It comes with a certain definition, certain emotions, certain expectations, certain things to do, etc.

Friend (Any relation i.e., Relatives etc.): If we call or treat someone as a friend then it comes with certain perceptions and we expect the other person to behave in the same way as the perception exists in society which we have influenced. So we just accept the society definition and we respond with the same emotions as perceived. Not only in the case of representations but also in other contexts or situations i.e., could be perceptions about colour, certain types of professions, certain types of attire, a certain style of speaking, a certain way of behaving, a certain way of appearance in particular places, exams and many more. **(We should change the perceptions so that we can change the reality because certain**

perceptions have their own negative effects which impact many people in a very negative way) Perception about something or some representation hinders us from thinking and acting objectively.

CHAPTER 5

TO THE READER

When I started writing this book, I had a doubt whether the reader would realize the importance of this content or not as it is essential that the reader should understand the content of the book and its importance. I was thinking further about what can hinder the reader from understanding this content so I started analyzing a similar scenario.

I always had these thoughts in mind when I was searching for a job i.e., Why I didn't put 100% effort into my placement preparation study during college? Even when professors said or when we had placement training, why didn't I realize the importance of placements?

So, I wanted to know the reasons why we don't understand or realize certain things at some point in time. I came up with a few possible reasons.

Firstly, I was influenced by the surroundings or circle and I didn't put 100% effort irrespective of people saying,

"You should study well so that you will get a good job." We always think that not doing any task is a neutral state but we should understand that when professors or well-wishers say to study and if we don't do that task then we actually are learning not doing that task i.e., in the opposite direction of what we wanted to do, our brain just learns it, it doesn't understand if it is a right or wrong, beneficial or non-beneficial.

Due to this when professors or placement officers told me to concentrate on placements, I didn't do it as already my brain had learned or was habituated to ignore it. Since it is habituated, our brain goes into **autopilot** mode (Autopilot mode is when it performs the activities or tasks unconsciously) and we automatically do our regular tasks.

For example, we know which way to go as soon as we enter our home.

To summarize, when you say or think of doing a task and if you don't do that task then you are actually learning to not do that task. So every time you don't do that task, it becomes more and more difficult to do the task.

Due to the above reasons, one may want to apply the concepts mentioned in this book but might fail to do because the person might have been in autopilot mode so it becomes difficult to understand or realize the importance of it at that time unless a good amount of effort has been put in.

So if you are not realizing the importance of these concepts then you should start analyzing them by applying these concepts in your life, go in-depth about it, and ask questions yourself, and then you will understand whether to adopt them or not. In case if you don't understand any part of this book then please read it again. The more you read, the better you will understand.

This content is very generic in nature apart from examples and hence is applicable to all irrespective of age group, culture, gender, etc. but one thing to remember is that, although each individual or group of individuals might be equally influenced, the proportion of impact it has on each individual and their family differs based on different classes of society, exposure and other factors due to which some readers may not appreciate this content at this point of time even after reading again. I would advise to keep this as a handbook and read it again when the need arises.

Some readers may realize the importance only when they have been affected by the influences mentioned here. They may then realize what proportion of impact has been made by the influences mentioned in this book.

Finally, I would say, whatever type of reader you may be, please make a note of these concepts and apply them accordingly.

CONCLUSION

Some might be aware of these facts or concepts mentioned in this book but may not tell others thinking what's the advantage of telling or maybe due to time constraints but I feel if we tell these concepts to others, it will, in turn, will help us i.e., the more we spread, the better we will make our surrounding which eventually helps our children and us as they will be influenced with the same surrounding.

Note: As mentioned earlier, for anything to happen in this world, it depends on many factors. Here I have focused on only one such factor i.e., the content we consume but I am sure, among others, this is a major factor that influences us.

"You may choose to ignore this but you can never say again that you did not know."

www.ingramcontent.com/pod-product-compliance
Lightning Source LLC
LaVergne TN
LVHW041600070526
838199LV00046B/2059